ONCE WHEN WE WERE YOUNG

P. CLAYTON HUGGINS

INKWATER
PRESS

PORTLAND • OREGON
INKWATERPRESS.COM

P. CLAYTON HUGGINS

ONCE WHEN WE WERE YOUNG

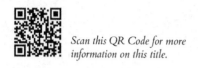

Scan this QR Code for more information on this title.

Publisher: Inkwater Press | www.inkwaterpress.com

Paperback
ISBN-13 978-1-62901-470-8 | ISBN-10 1-62901-470-2

Printed in the U.S.A.

3 5 7 9 10 8 6 4 2

DEDICATION

For The Nevis Writer's Group with gratitude.

CONTENTS

ACKNOWLEDGEMENTS

The author wishes to thank Carla Astaphan and Loughlin Tatem who read the manuscript and made suggestions.

Most of the poems were first read at The Nevis Writer's Group, which was founded by the author and Amba Trott (*Nonesense in Nevis 2005* ©) in 2006.

Many of the poems were given their first public reading at **Island Xpressions** in Basseterre, St Kitts.

I KNELT AT THE ALTER

I knelt at the alter.
The candles flickered
Along the path of love
And incense wafted

Aloft; tracing
A curlicue heavenward.
Here, my knees bend in
Supplication in the temple

Of love. Here, there is
No asking of forgiveness
No penance for love. She
Asks only that she be felt,

Be seen, be reverenced. You
laid on the alter, palms
heavenward as you
groaned a prayer to ecstasy.

Words reached and lost
our tongues as we uttered
unspoken prayers heavenward.
You reached for me and

held the wind as time
stopped to admire us.

Ah, love, bearing
the burden of this
lonely bed from the
alter of pain: carry

my heart aloft to
that place where
love lives in unbearable
ecstasy. Love forbids

us all but to worship
her in our lovely bodies.
Here we are: worshipful

and recumbent supplicants,
bearing the gifts of our
bodies for love's sake.

The ceremonies of love
fall away to reveal
nascent bodies templed
by acts of love and

thus it happens! The secrets
of sacred texts and hidden
practices shine in the
light of love.

I bow my head
and utter the wordless
prayer to love with
my tongue.

Here we are: acolytes,
enlightened by the
lights which guide from within;
knowing now that heaven

and all life lives within.
There is no temple but
our bodies, no truth but love.

SKIN DEEP LIE

You knelt at his bed

a jumbie bead
    rolling under your tongue

You thought
        it wouldn't go
    undone

as you whispered
    to his head.

You flittered around
        his body
in pretense of preparation,

but surely
        you did not think
that I would tell.

Heaven answers all our prayers:

did you ask
for tips
    from heaven;
has she smiled
through your hands?

You preferred to work
         alone
or to be surrounded
        by fools,
the better to appear
    all knowing.

Who knows your heart!

II

It was said
in jest
many betrayals ago,

but you have
held on
and made of
your skin
a prison.

You could not believe
that the truth
may be better,

and so have
made for yourself
a home
in which
everyday

you are reminded
that love does
not matter.

III

You held her
face in your
hands and
admired the skin;
though you could
feel in your heart
its
beauty, tissue thin.

Years of looking
had taught you
the truth of
that lie thrown
at you so
many heartaches ago:

You are beautiful!
But, you preferred
    another's lie
to your truth.

You have found happiness
in pleasing others but
have made of your heart
a prison for your
most ardent hopes.

IV

Come dear friend,
lets unlock your
heart and peer into
its depths. Look!

It beats for life
without regrets
    or fear.

Shall we follow
    its lead
or live in despair.

I KNELT AT THE TREE

I knelt at the
tree and uttered
a word to Heaven.

I wondered if you
    would hear

and guide me to that
place within,
    where
        you once
            lived.

I heard and then saw, what
      I had known only
          Dimly:

The arc of your
life left us in
    your wake

to ponder the depth
of your belief
and the strength
of your conviction.

It was deeply felt
and lived at an
intensity we were
too close to, not to
regard with nonchalance.
Did you find our
attention too distracting?

Did we give you enough
of what you needed to feel
at home within yourself?

"It covers a multitude of sins."

And, had we to tell the truth
would it not have
scorched our hearts to stone.

Such truths linger
on, even when we've
            passed.

They live on
as reminders
that the pain of
existence cannot
be avoided.

II

I feel in my heart
        an emptiness.
I know that doing
what's right will
not reward the
effort. We live,
dear one, amongst
others who despise
the world of the
heart and know
nothing of themselves
except what they
have been told.

Such pain
        cannot be avoided.

III

I knelt at the tree
and asked for guidance.
He bellowed that he was
            lost
and could not be helped.

My heart sang for despair
to find and comfort me.

I asked to be washed
in the blood of the lamb,
to be sanctified and
be made whole.

I waited
      for an answer
but heard
      only
the rustling of leaves.

THIS DAY

It came to me
that today; now;
shall never return.
I think of you and the
tree planted at your
head and know
that on your anniversary
I shall stand under
its cooling shade.

It rains, the leaves
drink their fill
and spit the rest
on the ground: to
water the roots
of our hearts.

I live now for that
day – we all do –
when we shall say:
yes, that was it,
I know now why
it had to be.

II

I saw you standing
on the sidewalk
your head made
distinguished by silver;
you held a book
in your hand
and looked quizzical.
I said: good day,
as I walked by.

III

I carried my thoughts
on my back and
wondered at their weight.

I heard the masqueraders
in the distance and
called out to you;
you answered but did
not know who.

The field seemed larger
than it should have been
and as I came to its
gate I rested in the
shadow of the cinder
wall and enjoyed the
relief of an emptying bladder.

IV

I had seen the Morris chairs
sitting alone in the office
and wondered if they were
known and still loved.

I knew them well, had
sat, slept and read on
them often enough.
They were loved and
cared for and supported
my burdened back
with ease: I sat and sank
into the folds of a thousand
fleeting memories as I
waited my appointment.

You were happy to see me
and flushed with enthusiasm and
self-assurance too. You were happy

to listen; share my thoughts.
I was grateful for your attention
and took it to be more than kindness.

V

You said that you weren't cut
out for domesticity; and
that guarded you, or so you thought,
from un-needed entanglements.

But, I noticed when we
met, your body came alive
though you stayed put. It
seemed natural for you:

to embrace a friend
on meeting – but why
I wondered, only girlfriends.
It seemed a touching
gesture, but was
freighted, just below
        its surface.

Your ungainly gait
        and your
volubility spoke
volumes about you.
Loneliness was a
constant companion
though you preferred
        solitude.

Come good friend,
let us sit and
enjoy the moment,
time has errands to
run and shall
leave us alone
to find our way home.

THE SUN WAS HOT

The sun was hot
And my bare head
Felt its touch. I
Walked along
The main road
Feeling at home
But not recognizing
Anyone. I walked
Past the old post
Office and wondered
Why, after forty
Years, it had not
Been rebuilt.
Its death had been final.
There would be no
Resurrection ceremony:
No celebration
Of its forgotten past;
Only this ruined
Reminder of our
Leader's hearts.

We wait, like
Slaves of old, to be
Told what to do,
Convinced that
In so serving, we
Obey a higher
Calling: content
To defend the
Illusion of order,
As we sit, unknowing,
Amongst the detritus
Of our ruined lives.
We live, but only
In the minds of those
Who hate us and

We're content to
Find only what is
Christ-like, in our
Obsequiousness. I turned
Away from the ruined
Walls and noticed that
The adjourning yard
Which once housed
A gas station and
Monkey, was a new
Event. There was no
Reminder in its painted
Walls, of the monkey
Show. No upper
Story to provide rest
From the mundane world.
Here it sits, a new bungalow,
Built on our frayed memories,
A poignant reminder
Of our intent: forget
It! You can't relive
The past! I walked on, refreshed,
Though not knowing how or why.

I came upon the old
Market and noticed the yard
Newly lawned. The old public
Cistern, the shed where ground
Provisions were displayed and
Imagined dinners settled and the
Public baths, where, if you
Preferred not to carry your water,
You could stand under a shower
And be carried away, at the
End of a hard day. I had stood
Many a Saturday morning;
Being squeezed tight, by large breasts,
As I waited for the butcher King
To ask me, what I wanted

And I would repeat the instruction: six pounds of meat!
He always remained
Quiet, the centre of the cacophony.
All shouted orders fell into a vat for
Noise. The harangue always left me silent.
Only Miss Mac didn't have to
Shout, she came and asked and was
Attended to promptly. No one
Protested: we did not believe
The seductive lies and fallacies
Spoken in democracy's name.
We knew and recognised Royalty
Among us.

Our Dowager reminded us
That we were of another
Time and place where hatred
And indifference were cause
For alarm and not the
Currency of our rulers.

I POINTED TO THE STARS ABOVE

No one cared.
I had shown my hand,
Confident that it meant
Something. But I alone
Saw what I did:
Nothing matters to those
Who do not care.
I pointed to the stars
Above. It was no mystery,
I could see the telltale
Signs and knew
The connection with my heart.
I told the story again
And again to anyone
Who would listen;
But, no one cared enough
To hide their disinterest.

This is the time. It matters
Now what it says. I hold
In my hand the past I knew
And cared for. I longed to
Feel at home among friends
Who remembered when.
No one did, nor cared enough.
I took the cue and walked away,
Looking to the stars for a sign
From my past; they watched,
Twinkling, as I reached
for the door, to the hall of sighs.

THE WRITER SINGS

There was no proscenium,
No hint of what was
To come, we sat, some
With baited breath
In anticipation:

What now of our
Lives would we see
Reflected here;

How would the scenes
From our lives be blocked.

The characters shunted
Their lives free of
Encumbrances and stood
For each of us.

We marveled at
Our complexities
Mirrored so lovingly.

You acted as though
You cared, you acted
As though you were mad.

Do those acts
Of inspiration leave
You free to contemplate
Old scenes from your
Life anew?

The words portray
The craft
As they betray
Your intent:

That others may come
To see and learn of themselves

In ways they could not
Have otherwise.

You stood in profile
And for a moment
I caught a glimpse
Of something I
Had not thought
Possible.

It left me in awe.
I closed the book
And folded my arms.

I looked at the children
Playing and wondered:
Would they remember
This day, this play; their
Roles.

We write our heart's
Stories and are usually
Surprised when the
Hero seems abstruse.

We know ourselves
Only because others
See us as we aren't.

We walk upon the stage
Ever hopeful that ours
Shall be the happy ending.
But, it rarely happens:
The stories
We write of ourselves
Are never edited by an
Indifferent hand.

We'd storm the stage
And create a drama
In which the

Hero lives our
Hopes and dreams
And fights on to
The bitter end.

The writer acts,
But in fact, the writer
Sings: we hum each
Day the melody of our
Lives. It draws us to
That place within where
Life is knotted together
Out of our fancies and whims.

I AIM TO PLEASE

Here is your aim to please
The one which gets you there
And here is the indifference
It breeds and the: "I don't care"

Here is the gratitude
You expected, wrapped
Tight in the pleasures of
The flesh; it wasn't your wrath

Which stopped me
But the pain buried
Deep within your chest.
His words curried

Favour with your heart and
Bound it deep, in the dark. Here
Is the love you missed
When he let slip: "I don't care"

Here are the eyes swollen shut
The pain which floated free.
Here is the heart out of which drained
All hope, caring and ecstasy.

Here it lies, a broken wreck
Beached on regret's heartless shore
Here, across its bow pain had
etched: *I was not the whore.*

Here is the question you did not ask
Whose answer is steeped in misery:
Why did you bother to take my heart;
When all you wanted, was to fuck me?

Here is the certainty you felt
That your heart was made for pain.
Here are the opportunities lost
When you cried again and again:

I don't care! It was not
Your fault that you fell
So deeply. Only love
Can tell Heaven from Hell.

You can feel that difference and
Know it deep within. Now, can
You rest your hand upon your heart
And say: Here, I don't care.

UNTITLED SONNET
(ON READING SHAKESPEARE WHILE SPEAKING TO A FRIEND)

You were just another Shylock
Backing out to save your skin.
Your heart was the deal struck
But you thought giving that much, a sin.
No one'd taught you when you were young
That it doesn't matter as long as it's done
                                        with respect.
You just thought they all had to be wrong:
Even when they said, I love you; it seemed in
                                        jest.
Now it pains you to feel
So you live the lie you've proven.
'Though you've bound your heart with
                threads of steel
You wonder why it won't be forsaken.
    And you will know it is in loving
    That we learn that love is for giving.

THE DOVES PLAY

The doves play at fighting;
They spring their wings and grab
A tight circle to show
How it's done:
You flounce up; but do not
Shed a tear nor lose a
Feather. That is how real
Wars are fought; how they're won!
We argue, but never
Once would we circle back
To show our feathers.
We'll peck away at our
heart, make of it a
Scab, even when we get
To blood, we continue
On, never circling:
Always this bickering.
We smash against the pull
Of contentment, never
Stopping to wonder why.
We see around us the
Hints, but never connect
What we see to what we
Know. It's thus that we learn
How it's done: the constant
Repetition, the dread
Of boredom, which follow
Us to the bitter end;
Never asking, never
Wondering. Like the doves,
We live without reason:
They though, can fly away.

READING

We read the texts to gain knowledge.
The texts read our minds and foil them:
Closing off the fields of delight
That would guide us home; by sinking
The lies, floating between the lines.

Long years of schooling had left me
Advanced in the eyes of the world:
I wore the robe of the doctor,
Had claimed the clenched jaw of prestige
And dead respectability;

At least, that's what I have now found
Shimmering on the horizon,
As I drift along on a sea
Of complacency, with no star
To guide, but fear of ennui.

I bustle about in my robe
'though I know it's to hem and haw
But, I wrest from time's obstinate
Hand, a brilliant moment, to
Delight, in reading my own mind.

A LIGHT, A DROP OF WATER

You walked off of the pier
Accompanied, but you were
Alone: no one could see the
Fissures in your heart

You had tried many times
To climb out of yourself,
But found the going slippery.

Your tears had daubed the
Sides of your prison walls
And pain had jailed you
From your heart.

You had been told that
It wouldn't last.
You had come to believe
There could be no hope
For you.

You tried so many times
To give up the game, but
Always, something held you back:
A light, a drop of water. Something
In your heart, held you fast to the
Spot and kept you transfixed.

You had, like many of us
Learned to cry yourself to sleep
But found on waking the same
Damp walls of your heart.

Oh, the loneliness, the pain
Of not knowing, of not feeling.

A sip, a puff, took you away
From the pain, but never
Far enough to not feel.

A NEED FOR SPACE

FOR SHELLY CROSSE

It is not an apology, but
An acknowledgement of your
Need for space.

The fine sand
Seeps between your
Toes, as you walk the beach
In your runners and try to
Hold your soul deep within.

It's been a hard few days
And they will get better,
But not before the sea
Hides your tears
And clears your throat.

The scissors bird circles above
And remind you, in a way that melts your heart, that
Love is eternal, if always out of reach.

I follow along in your wake, tacking
Back and forth; reaching for the gust
That will take me away from this scene,
But, and I don't quite understand why,
I keep tacking back to your course: we
Keep sailing away to each other.

The walk, then the run on the beach,
Gets you up and alive, then the reminder
Comes from islands away to call you back
To that place you were happy
To have fled. He reaches for you
And you watch, as he grasps at what's
No longer there and are happy that now,
After all that, you can regard his efforts
With indifference.

I feel deep in my heart a spot: soft
Inviting, as hard as diamonds
Where I keep the memories of you
Arranged in a knowing disorder.
They remind me why loyalty can
Never be over-valued.

And here your heart lies and sings
And rocks and floats and cries
And knows itself better than
You can ever know.

I'll come and sit with you.
Hear your heart speak truths
Your tongue cannot utter and
Linger on your words like
The skin to my flesh.

You teach me in many ways
That words will salve the heart,
As you stand alone
On the shore in the gusts of morning,
With nothing to remind you of
Who you are, but the silence
Of your open heart.

A CALMING BREEZE

You braced against the window,
Aching to escape the grasp
Of the hands which held you fast
To that spot. Yes, you were old
Enough to know it would be
Wise to not let him reach you,
So, you yielded to the force
Of his touch. You relented
Only when he moved along,
Taking with him the indifference
You felt in his heart. It could
Have broken you, rubbed you in
Ways you would not have cared for.

Today, you are happy for
The new Sun: you sit languid
And forlorn, waiting for what
Today or tomorrow shall
Bring. I look at you and watch
As you sway to the calming
Breeze. Grateful for his changeable ways.

EXPECTATIONS

You sat welcomed at the edge of the bed
I touched your back and felt you melt away.
Was the embered fire which burns within
Not bright enough to hold your attention?
Yes, I had learned long ago that such flames
Can be fanned, the fires stoked, the pot boiled.

I had learned to have my expectations
Met, and that on my terms; terms that I have
Come to expect are hardly ever met.
And yet the strings once pulled taut now run slack:
The heartless gesture slips through my fingers
And the grace of acquiescence has fled.

Look how the Scissors bird floats on thin air,
Its wings spread full to cover the distance
Between here and there. Oh! It looked askance
But did not move. It stopped without a care.

I lingered awhile and saw what it did:
And I cried when I saw I could not fly;
Though for you, we both know, my heart will soar.

I HAD THOUGHT MY HEART CLOSED

There it sits, a blue square.
A reminder of a time that was.
I had hovered over this patch
For years, unbeknownst to anyone
I'd kept it hidden as though
It were a secret: but hidden from whom?
It made of my heart, a sarcophagus
And, came In time to block the light within.
My heart shone, but dimly.

The doves sang to me.
The wind caressed my soul.
There were a thousand raindrops
Of warning, but I held fast:
Convinced that if I acted the
Part, I could persuade others to
Join me as I sang:

No, my heart is dead.

I could no longer feel.
But, buried as deep as they are,
Feelings, although denied,
Will always live on, to remind us
Of our inner truths.

You offered to clean for me:
You assessed in that one look
Into the plastic bag with the soap,
What had to be cleaned, what
Needed to be done. But, I would
Not have guessed in a thousand
Heartbreaks, that you would pull
Apart and clean my heart with such ease.
You left me standing with none
Of my once comforting defenses.

I could not claim the horror
And delight of falling in love
Or of rejecting you; pushing
You away, as you'd said.

It's that I found in your
Presence, I stood without
Defense and found to my
Surprise, that I needed no
Props, no crutch to bear me up.
I searched for the usual clues,
But the cloudless sky shone
No light my way. The stars
Were neutral (though they held us
Days apart). The doves, silent,
Flew by and my heart, laid bare
Could no longer be hid.

You, so effortlessly, with such purity
Left me unhinged from myself.

And, I stopped dead when I saw
Myself as I had not, for years:

I had forgotten that long ago
I had made a pact – under duress
That, I would act the part
But not become that part.
That the pain of duress could
Be blanched by bending, to
Avoid breaking; to separate the
Inner truth I knew, from the
Public lie I proffered.

I had acted the priest
To placate the holy father.
But held fast in my heart
The one I knew myself
To be, before induction.

My dear sweet heart
Who cried on this pillow
Leave your scent as
Proof that it did happen:
That my heart which had been
Once cold, once dead; half
Forgotten under the blue square,
Can feel, that it can sing, can fly.

You laid upon your back,
Your breasts moonlit and
Pliant to the aches of desire
And longing. The secrets
You held were revealed as
We entwined. You held
My heart close and wondered for
Days after, at the depth of
Passion you had pulled from me.

II

You sensed within, the ease
Of kindred spirits. You wondered
At the possibilities that here,
You might have met someone
Worthy of your heart.

You had grown tired
Of feeling empty
After being comforted
And your heart, so rich,
Yearned to share its wealth
With someone who would
Touch your very soul.
I wonder at the possibilities
And wait patiently – observing –
For my heart to speak to me;
To tell me what I sensed already.

JUST WHEN

Just when I thought it was at an end
You upped and called my name
Just when I thought you were my God-send
I realized it did not matter why it was all the same

We said goodbye at the Café
You, lost amongst friends
Of convenience. I, wondering
Why I was there

The gin lasted longer than the night
I saw you close the gate on me
And knew then it was at an end

There was no room for pretense
though truth wore a gaudy dress to
Hide the pain

My heart turned to stone when it
Was plain to see
You cared but never loved

I am grateful for all the tender mercies
You showed me, less so for the venom
You spat my way. I had flattered myself
That it was all for some good

IT NEVER ENDS

The clouds skitter along the sky.
Boasting, running, roiling. The
Ground is wet from laughter.
And here, between the sheets,
It's damp. We roll like the clouds,
Passing fast, before stopping
Halts the play.

I hold you, like the wind, in my mouth
And feel you fly away. Your words
Are silent as we speak a tongueless
Language: who will stop the rain…
We live each day as it comes.
The rain rolls off the roof
And falls with indifference on my hopes.
We laughed now at this rain,
But knew that ours was yet to come.
Just yesterday, it seemed that it
Could all end in peace: that none
Of this would matter; it never ends:
The not knowing: that's how hope
Is born.

Your tears fell from the sky and we
Looked on as you mourned for our past.

There is something in the air, a subtle
Learning, an expectation, that we shall
Be revealed.

CEMENT STEPS

The cement steps are hard under my feet.
I walk on, feeling the effort in my
Tight muscles. I came here to find respite
From knowing you: Hum our past to rest.
I watch out on the blue grey sea, a white
Winged boat sailing. It keeps me company.
You and I were the only ones: we had
Sailed together, buffeting seas as we
Rode the waves home. We never cried. There was
Always someplace new to sail when we got
To port and the urgency to leave, the
Lightness of the moment, impelled our journey.

I had heard it well before: you loved the
uncertainty of sailing without a
Rudder, the void your only guide. I had
Followed along in your wake, hoping to
Reach you; hoping to make home in your heart.

You buried your head in my chest, pushed hard
And then told the story of how it is
That what you do lives on always, always
For others to deal with. I had longed for
A respite from the not knowing, from the
Fury and doldrums. So, I find myself
Here, far from the sea, my palm sailing atop
Weathered bricks, as I walk these cement steps.

THE GREEN GRASSHOPPER

The green grasshopper flew around me
And I listened to the song it sang.
I knew what I heard, but I pretended –
I loved the mystery of not knowing.
In the meeting room the radio played a song
I did not know, I loved the pain in the
Singer's voice. I listened as she floated into
The distance and the green grasshopper,
Flew this away.

I felt the cold air on my skin,
I asked if she enjoyed singing.
I asked if being a professor in Middlesex
Was rewarding. She looked at me, then
Looked away. She thought then, I wasn't
Worth it.

I asked the question because I wanted to
Know. She heard questions which were
Not being asked and drifted away to that
Place in her mind where she loved
Herself and could be alone.

I sat up and kissed your precious body.
I knew that you had lied. You knew what
You had done, but it was easy for you
To hide from yourself. That had become
Easy for you: the lying.

That was when we learned to
Laugh with the shadows that lived
In the corner of our eyes.

SHEATHED IN SILENCE

You wore a cross on your forehead
The fire burnt deep in your heart
I wonder at times if it's worth
Asking: how did we come this far?
I do not know, they cannot say;
The answers are sheathed in silence.
All I know I must sing to you,
Fall on my knees, if that would do

I pray to the sea for guidance
And hear her whispered silk: it's you…
You said my words made you complete,
Filled your heart's bowl with love's soft dew.
We were both told, we would meet here
To find our purpose for living.
I'll shoulder your cross in my heart
And be happy, for now: it starts.

AN OBSCURE BOOK

FOR TYNISHA CAMELITA

It was an obscure book
written to souls now lost.
I had to sail my memory
And it came up a lost cause.
My fingers splayed the waves
To find the familiar words,
I had misplaced them somewhere
But heard them, still, in my head.
The people had sinned
Or so it had been taught,
For the words offered were
Full of redemptive thoughts.

If you must live, do it right!
And think only on those
Things that shine bright.
If it is pure, of good report,
If it is of virtue and sung praise.
That keeps well, in your heart.

You did, my dream, gift me
These stern words, written for the
Long dead tribe, when all
I wanted was for your heart
To open me wide.

I kneel and say the words,
But nothing comes, my lips
Are parched and dry. My
Words float away to an empty sky.

I wanted you more than words can say:
I'd read and sing for life. My words
On lambent tongue were not prayed
For a lie.

You offered me these long dead
Words, as a sop to my fervent heart.
I took them in and hung them bright,
To repeat in the dead of dark:

Whatsoever things are pure
If there be virtue in your heart
Let it find love and be at rest.

THE SOUL STEALERS

Stepping on stones your
Long white dress
Caught in your
Left hand, you waved
The other for balance;
To catch yourself

As you avoided the water
Which ribbed around the
Moss dressed stones. How
You did not slip? We watched
From the shore, the black
Sand cradling our unshod
Feet. The air was still and
The Sunlight sat upon us,
Silent, insistent, waiting for
Someone of us to let go.

Our breaths were held in
Anticipation: would you slip,
Would you fall, would you
Fly away or would you walk

On. Everyone here had come
To see you. We had heard the
Stories, they had been told
Since our grand-mother's
Time. They said you had
Slipped from a ship, others
That you had been thrown
Overboard. That you had
Made to catch a falling baby
And that you too went
Floating. It was the
Stories that held us fast,
Waiting to see you here.

II

She pirouetted and swiveled
On the ball of her foot.
She let her skirt fall from her
Hand and floated up, her
Skirt billowing as she kicked
Her legs as though swimming.

She slowly disappeared into
Thin air: first her head, then
Her shoulders all the way
Down, as if she were crossing
An invisible line, down to
Her white shoed feet.

III

On the beach, a thin boy
In brown bathing trunks
Noticed that out on the
Horizon a sailing boat
Disappeared at the same
Time as the woman. He
Was the only one to notice
The boat and woman, but
Did not know it then.

He thought that everyone else
Was like him: that they saw
What he could, that they felt the
Light which shone behind
Everything, the way he could.

IV

He noticed and wondered why
His grand-mother looked at
Him like that when he told
Her what he had seen. He
Did not understand then, why.

She held him close and placed
His head on her ample bosom.

He thought she liked him,
She always gave him sweets.

He did not know that she
Knew that he would have
To be protected; hidden out
In the open, less he be
Found out and the soul
Stealers came to ask, to
Take him for their game
Of hide and seek.

DEPTHS UNKNOWN
FOR LEAH CRAG-CHADERTON

And yet, when we spoke, you did not say.
We danced around the point, you wanted to
Go and I would have followed, but we
Stayed. We stood on the beach alone, the
Waves caressing our feet, holding us
Fast to the spot. You hid your eyes behind
Tortoise shell rims, the ones you said made
You look pretty, you liked them. You wore
Rings on your thumbs. Sometimes, when you
Were reading and they caught your eye you
Would stop: your eyes swimming from the words
To the rings to the words. They held you
In place, though your heart would float free.

Your lips, two roses held close, parted
In a smile when you spoke. "She looks
Intelligent" is what they always
Said about you. You were pretty but
Coursing through your heart were depths unknown

You lived as though washed in respect, you
Looked unapproachable, cold, aloof.

But looks can kill and yours killed stares of
Indifference. Even as a little
Girl, they called you: Miss. It held you in
Check, somewhere between respect and
Solitude. You bantered with yourself,
Trying to find a space in your heart,
In your mind, where the room was round
Enough to hold you. You wished you were
Shorter, you wanted your hair to be
Longer, but these were asides, you knew
The truth: it told a story which you
Loved because it called your beauty, true:

And you knew it too...

THAT'S ALL THERE IS

If that is not the answer –
Then what is?

I had thought that it
      Would not matter:

That as long as the
Right thing was being
Done, that all would
Be forgiven. That
They would understand.

I walked along the narrow
Ledge, knowing that I
Would not fall.
That if I did, I would be caught.

Now I find myself at
The end of my way.

There is an abyss ahead
And nothing I have learned,
None of the thousand steps
I had taken in my journey,
Prepared me for what
Was to come.
What is my next step,
What am I to do?

The darkness is deep.

I stood with my back and both palms
Against the wall and
Placed one foot over the
Edge, but dared not walk
Off. One last settling
Of my faith.

I swim in hope of
Catching the light.

I struggle against the
Current, I soar, I plunge
I fight to keep above
The surface: to breath
Golden air.

I fall and swoop below
My limits, but float to
The surface every time.

There is hope, there is always hope
Sometimes, that's all there is.

LIVING DREAMS

I don't listen when you call,
Though I pay attention
To what you say. I hold
My breath, but not for you.

I hear what you say
But wonder why

Your words and actions
Live so far apart.

Your words create living dreams
But I'll wait for you to wake

Before I say…

SALT POND
(THE FIRST WEDNESDAY IN SEPTEMBER)

As I drive pass the Great Salt Pond,
I notice the grand stone houses
Hugging the side of the hills,
Reclining in the soft amber sunset,
Their feet, stretched to the water's edge.
These majestic houses, were far from
Community. They were built on
Hope and the certain knowledge
That they would find lithe mushay
Bodies, to keep their walls
From falling silent.

II

The glass windows, expansive,
Were tinted against the Sun's
Prying eyes – and native curiosity.

They would come, filled with the bilge
Of empire and ambition, with no
Certainties, but those which enforced
Its own laws of cease and desist.

III

Somewhere in Newtown, a woman,
Whose children bring only occasional
Happiness, will one day make the daily
Pilgrimage to this hill, to serve and protect
The wash from the wake of Empire
From eroding the stance and glares
Of envy, That Empire affords.

She will learn in time to see through
The tinted blue dolly baby eyes
And, if she is lucky, chuckle at the
Pain of those who own but can not have.

IV

A bright: good morning! Sung
To insincerity's garish smile,
Begins the day in this fulsome pile.
How are your kids? That stung.

It was not that she asked:
How could she not, for a pittance, purchase
A silence that would float free here and chase
Away truth's stinging asp.

V

Newtown arrives to work
And sees in the expanse
Of glass and rubbled stone
A mordant reminder
Of her grandmother's past
And grandchildren's future:
It wouldn't be the first time
Since Buckley's fitful morn
That we'd have to find,
Bottle and stone to match.

DIAMOND STUDDED LEAVES

Diamond studded leaves…
It was a moonlit night.

She had whispered something.
He knelt closer to hear.

She kissed and held his head
Between both palms and sighed:

It was so beautiful;
They looked like diamonds.

The stars, veiled by moonlight,
Snuggled against the sky.

He hummed and counted all
That steered a course his way:

Her eyes, her lips, her breasts;
Her warm soulful body.

No no, today today…
It rained from a blue sky

And my heart sang to me:
Diamonds, diamonds

Falling from a clear sky.
It made me think of you.

THERE WERE HINTS

I

There were hints, there were suggestions.
I saw the writing on the wall.
You said, I would be your future;
A June visit, but then, that call.

You were moving too fast, she said.
You had known her since all girls school.
She reminded you of your crush
And tied your heart with envy's spool.

You had set the table so well.
We would feast on love's ripe portions.
But, a simple question, unmasqued;
Would signal love's abnegation.

II

She planted in your heart, where once
Love grew, a seed. She knew how well
To exact revenge for the years
Of pain, which left her heart a swell:

Racing to crash against the cold
Shores, of your rude indifference.
She held your heart and made of it
A doubt filled vitrine; the inference

Being: no love! "Do you know yourself"?
The impossible question, that
Stops and makes of us all, doubters:
Blind fools, who'd see love as a trap.

III

Oh, my heart sings, full of your love.
It asks only that it be held;
That your feelings not be left prone
To fall prey, to doubts' deadly spell.

Oh, why! Oh why would doubt medal?
This race is won at love's behest!
You were told you would be transformed
And consented to pass that test.

Now, she is righteous and you, lost:
The dark recesses of your mind
A baleful, shallow, charted sea.
Now, my heart sinks, full of your love.

FOR YOU, FOR ME

You said: I'm sorry; so, I forgave you.
The cut had been so deep, it drew marrow.
Oh love! I had cried: how long must we wait.
Oh love! I had cried: how deep must we go

To know: is it love that curses our lives
To swirl around in eddies of dull pain?
Oh love! How long must we wait not to feel.
Tell me now, is it true that you do lie?

Oh love, oh lovely love, tell my heart now:
When will it know that your words say what's true.
I want to know, more than my eyes can tell,
That the heart can feel its way out of love;

A love that sings of its pain, that can sing
In its own knowing way, of the way home.

IT IS BRIGHT OUTSIDE
(FOR TCS)

It's bright outside.
The light flickers
In your heart now.

We had sat for hours,
Counting out the stars
As the earth kept time.

We had tried to find
A place to call home,
But time would only

Allow us our hands.
We ate our hearts full
At our pillow wide

Table and the distance
Tance between here and
There, marked our way home.

II

A love that falls by
The wayside, will grow
Amongst the shrubbery,

For though we may mark
Time, stamping in place
As we live this spot,

It is our heart's beat,
That guides our quick march
Along this wayside.

III

You wore the pink
To match the black
Pant, the one you

Said made you look
Younger. You stooped
To catch the words

And I saw in
Your eyes, the light
Of hope scatter

Across the leaf
In a thousand
Symbols that sang

Your life into
Being.

IV
You pulled away
Easier than
You had ever
Done before, you

Found it in your
Heart to let go,
To float away
On your sea of

Blue happiness.
You fell silent
And watched from the
Door of your open

Heart, the shadows
Of time slip by.
You placed your hand
Upon your heart.

V
I prayed for you.
Asked for Heaven's
Blessings. I had

Seen how knowing
You would show us
Both to her gate.

Your eyes sees all,
Melt cold hearts, your
Lips, pursed as they
Are, hold your tongue
From the stinging
Barb. None but the
Thoughtful, can slip
By your open heart..

TO SURPRISE AND DELIGHT

The lines tell a story of form
And volume, of shapes and of
Things to come.

Here, the pencil traces a curve
Which signs of a time when
This shape defined and comforted.
It bent to my will and told
A truth otherwise hidden.

The colours are muted, they
Take the shape of the forms.
Revealing in hues subtle and
Otherwise, the ways in which
Life bends to our delight
And curious whims.

This hand, which shapes these
Lines, covers a space in my
Mind, to which I return – you in tow –
Where the forms and shapes live.
Waiting for that peculiar urge;
To come forth, to
Surprise and delight!

I HEARD LAUGHTER

I heard laughter, it was floating from the hill
I tried to catch the joy, the air was still

He watched me turn his way, the Sun was bright
He was laughing at us. It served you right

He mused: I wish someone would take me down
Wet my parched lips, kill me now, let me drown

The pain is hard to bear, my blood is dry
For all this and more; O father, let me die

2

I turned a corner on myself to catch
The pain floating on the wind, I would latch

On to the tears and thus become trapped by
Love. I wanted to heal, to stop the lie

From seeping out, all he wanted were scared
Hearts for his goat-headed master who stared

His dead blue eyes empty. For all his might
He lived in fear that he would be found out

THE ARC

The arc bent my way
　　　　or so I thought.

It had all been written in
　　　　　　the stars

Ordained by Heaven,
　　　　it would do, so well.

But time had stamped it:
　　　　leaves blowing in the wind.

SHIFTING GROUND
(FOR SERENITY)

I knelt and tied a bow on your ankle

It kept your shoe tight and in place

You felt my hand on your flesh and wondered...

It touched in ways you had not expected
You felt the ground shift beneath your worn heart

Oh don't, oh don't, oh don't: get up...(you whispered)

YOUR LONELY HEART

And when the lights
Went out, you sat up;
Surprised that you
Could now see what
Was in the dark.

You rubbed your eyes
And called out. I answered
But you heard nothing
In the dark. You floated
Away from yourself
Watching for any hint
Of what was to come.
You were not surprised
To see yourself still
Young there, as you
Floated away.

I caught your lonely
Heart on my tongue
And spoke it to
Life. You said:
I love you, I said
I love you. But,
We will always float
Our separate ways.

WE LIGHT NEW STARS

The grave Sun, sets on a distant star.
The heart floats away to find its home.
You and I were once tied together.
Time has shifted; so, we stand apart

From the familiar, as we gather
The sparks from our hearts, no more to roam.
Time has collapsed, all comes untethered.
We are all now here, to light new stars.

GENTLE EMBRACE

Wait until midnight, that's when it ends.
She will hold a flower to her heart
And tell you with her smile, yes, it's right.

Leave that moment until she comes home.
You will see in her eyes, in her lips
That flame she lit, that will never die.

Come sweet love, it's now we bind our hearts.
Distance turns to ash in love's full glare
And leaves us close, in gentle embrace.

I had thought it done, a thing to miss.
Now, I stop and marvel at love's wit:
She teaches and guides our paths with grace.

HOUSE OF A THOUSAND DREAMS

I slid into the back seat.
The black leather felt cold
    against my palm.
I settled my body into the
Space once reserved for
       dignitaries.

You slid in beside me
And said something
    I could not hear.

I did not care.

I rested my hand on
Your thigh and felt
your body sigh.

Up ahead, a red light blinked.
It guided us to the place we
       once knew.

The gloved hand steered us
To the house of a thousand dreams.

We opened ourselves to its welcoming
        walls.
They were blue, with a hint of pain.
I folded myself around a corner
And came upon my past.

You sat alone
In the fading light,
Red dots for pupils;
The bed was unmade.

You said it was futile.

I saw in your perfectly
Coifed hair a past I
Had outlived.

Your lips, so perfectly
Shaped then, I now realized
Had remained young and lifeless.

I said goodbye as
I opened the door.
Yesterday will never
Be the same.
I turned off the light,
But, did not lock the door.

BEHIND THE SHADOWS

I had watched as you sank
Behind the shadows.
Days later we would wonder
And make a mystery of the
Simple observation. We search
For signs in the sky; hoping that
What we feel in our hearts does
Shine on in the light of distant stars.

The clouds were gray, the sky
Sombre-dark, the wind sheathed
Us in its hot breath.

It wasn't something we hadn't seen
Or felt before, but the possibilities
Kept us engaged.

We saw meaning in
The gray-reflected sea
And shapes of things
To come in the
Floating clouds.

The searching heart
Longs to find an echo
For its hopes and
Will alight on distant
Stars and stumble in
Its own darkness
To hear the answers
To its gentle pleadings.

TIME WILL SIT BESIDE ME

I had thought that all was lost.
I had looked to my right
But could see no light.
It was that my past was crossed

Off. I fumbled in the dark.
I found what I had been
Looking for,
But it was not my heart.

I looked to my left
     and saw the light.
It left me in its shadow
To seek what I had left

Behind. Now, I sit alone
     on the shore,
The waves beating at my feet;
Though it's hard to tell,
I know my heart's asleep.

Perhaps a drink will sooth the pain,
But I know from sad experience
     that it isn't so:
I'm just another lost soul
     marking time,
Trying hard to avoid the so

What! Living a lie in silence.
But, it won't be for long...
Though it's cold and lonely
I can see the sky slowly

Turning blue, time will
     sit beside me
As we wait out this
     dread feeling.

I'LL ASK FOR NOTHING MORE

The Sun strikes the face
And Winter melts away
I walk atop these cobbled
Stones and my heart says:
Here; it knows the way.

I lie in bed listening;
The rain caresses the leaves
And leave them thirsting
For more. 'though it's midnight
The sun shines bright somewhere
So I'll ask for nothing more.

BELIEVE

What else can we do but shop
What else can we do but stop
Our lies guided us yesterday
But my heart says the truth is here
    to stay

May as well let it pass
We'll shape the future someday
Who knows now how long this shall last
All I know is the Sun shines today

I'll tuck my shirt in
Straighten the tie my father wore
I'll kneel and confess all my sins
Be done and worship Gods no more

In Gaza, the dead raise stone bouquets
To remind us of our solitude
The bullets were shaped for sockets
To open the eyes of the ruled

No one wanted to believe
We were anything but good
So the quiet death of will
Was accepted where we stood

It was as plain as our heart's blank leaf
That all the havoc done in our name
Had returned to us unleashed:
Ravenous, rabid, bloodied, deranged.

I peered into the gathering dark
And heard the voices of the millions dead
They screamed: we're yours; as they took
    my heart
Drank my spirit for water then broke my heart
    for bread.

WHAT ELSE IS THERE TO DO

Were you testing me
Were you teasing me.

You said it couldn't be
But you held me and guided
My body into the intimate
Corners of ecstasy

"You're over me" they said
So I sent you my love:
What else could I do.

Was it my performance
I should have known
When you said you would
Find me a girlfriend, (next week)
What else could I do

You were testing me
I failed to impress
For that I am truly sorry,
But not much, because I
Love you and always will.
What else can I do.

I do not have the answers
Because I do not know the truth
Am just a lover doing
What it takes to love you
What else can I do

I live to see your heart
Lifted high above the crowd
Being loved and loving.

What else is there to do.

TAKE MY HEART

I struggle with all my might
I fight to win the good fight
I labour in a field of my own design
Blinded by love, I didn't see the sign

You took me home to show me your heart
I found it hanging in your closet
It floated amongst your memories
Bound in a blood-stained corset

I turned in the light to see more clearly
You lying in the bed beside me
Come let's find a reason to be here:
Let's go to the depths for ecstasy

I wanted more than you were
                        willing to give:
a depth of feeling; the pain of honesty.
Useless, meaningless sex
were the gifts you offered knowingly.

You wanted the pleasure
Without feelings.
I've tried, but find empty
            coupling
A useless treasure

You'll give it one more chance
For you know deep within
its emptiness and will dance
To fill your heart with meaning

Come my love
Take my heart
And learn how
To hear its pleadings.

THE WITHERED TRUTH

You valued your
daughter's plumage
silk black it was
but golden to you
who could see only
the path she should take.

Her heart was hers
but who'd win it.
You knew better and
had tasted the sweat
of years of betrayal:
smiles which only
bare the teeth; laughter
which cuts the heart;
and the pat on the back
which daubes fear.

All of this you knew
and could protect her from:
and men! Love and admiration
were crazy talk.

You knew after five
children and many
other betrayals that it
was not worth it, but
you held on in hope;
the disappointments of
a lifetime would not be
forgotten and it would
show in the plumage:
they'd know what not
to do.

You saw a sloop
on the horizon, (the
blue sea silvered by
the noon Sun), it

would come ashore
or sail straight: you
would make sure
that its hold
on you would be
fleeting. It peeled
away the sea and
leant against the wind,
its sails drunk with
breeze. You hated the
unexpected and so saw
all that could go wrong:
what if it sank, capsize;
or ran aground. Her
plumage would get wet!

You closed your eyes
and danced in the hot sand
to mark your sadness.
Her plumage would remain
dry and her heart pure.

You sought in your bitterness
to protect her from her heart.
You scuttled her hopes along
with yours so that her plumage
would remain ever near you.
You would look at it and
admire its brilliance but not
see its withering.

You were convinced that
you were saving it for
something better, but that
was just it: you knew no
better, so did not know
when to let go.

Your daughters shall follow
you and know your loss, and
shall come to know your
unhappiness and bitterness
as well as you.

You value your daughters
Plumage, more than they.

GOLD DUST

We'll walk pass the Ghettoes
And float towards the sky
We'll leave this world behind
It's no longer our sty

Just when it seemed beyond reach
It crossed closer than before
I ran from Heaven to tell
Them about the end, the score

It was never about Him
It was just his crucifix
It was never meant to end
Until we drowned crossing Styx

It was never when
It was never thus
He preached he could turn
Our tears to gold dust.

BLUE BUTTERFLIES

No one here stands on ceremony
Though we observe the pieties
It was just as well it didn't stop
Our lives were hemmed by niceties

We floated above the surface
Never stopping to gather dust
It was thus we came late to learn
What to believe, whom not to trust.

It was never about Jesus
He was just the chosen patsy
It would never end in rapture
Some get lost finding ecstasy

It lasted an eternity
Or so it seemed in the end
It was his back against the cross
That whipped heaven, told us when

The blue butterflies
Flew against the sky
They were swallowed by heaven
It no longer matters why we try.

LOVE IS THE OBJECT

You'd laid on your side
Your back against the world
It had been a welcomed
Rest from the pain you felt
In your heart. You had tried
Countless times (to what end)
To stop the feelings and
Had grown tired of the
Effort. You couldn't stop
Your feelings, but you could
Get rid of the object.

But why are you confused?

You stepped into the rain
Wearing a purple dress
And shrouded tight by a
Parasol. You sought to
Bring me down but was too
Blinded by your anger.
It hurts to feel! But that's
Life. Your empty heart bleeds
Advice. 'Though it can be
Taken this or that way
Love is still the object.

THE HAMMER

The hammer falls and yes, night begins
You stood at the door and saw it all
Who will go with me to learn the truth
To know the answers before they call

The hammer beats to dust in my heart
The fear I once felt of being in love
These are the blows we'd take willingly
To beat our fears into the white dove

I had hammered hard at your closed door
The answers we sought I thought were there
Those illusions are most blindly held
That'd set our minds free if we dare

The hammer falls and yes: thus it ends
What was at the door now lives within
No one's keeping score, we know that now
It's the hummingbird that walks on air

HEARD IT ALL

I saw it all
But did not believe
It came at me
With wings aflutter
Come with me now
If you wish to live.
I am alive
But you may not die

I heard it all
But could not see how
Not dying now
Would not set me free.
Your goal is set
And it must be met
Kneel before me
And rise a free man

I did it all
Now am floating free
High above, oh
How I understand
Now: it was in
Submission that I
Came to know that
What had me was fear.

THE RIGHT TIME

There was nothing new to be said,
We had heard it all before.
But, the time was right
So our words ran off
Deep into the night.

We'd not recall any of this,
It wouldn't be important anyway.
It was just the moment,
That made for
Idle conversation.

TO HEAL MYSELF

I'd turn my back on what I knew
Shared the secrets of my heart
What can I say now but that
I knew the truth from the start

It dealt my heart a heavy blow
To know that I'd live with the regrets
And yet I ran boldly into oblivion
And tasted bitterness

I'd forgotten I knew how
To play the fool,
The thought that I would
Lose you
Kept me beating against the door

Open I cried to my heart
It heard, but did not reply

It said it knew now
When I obeyed and
When I strayed:

I'll come here, to heal myself.

IF IT WASN'T LOVE

It wasn't love:
I knew all the lines
They were well rehearsed
I knew too my heart
Was well closed.
I had been warned
But I was thirsty:

I saw on your cup
The marks of all
The men who had
Gone before me
And so I closed
My eyes and
Drank my fill.

I heard your sigh
As I eased upon
Your thighs

You held on long
Enough to catch
My attention
You held
Your cup steady as I drank.

I would remember your
Many kindnesses
And in gratitude washed
Your cup and turned it up
To drain dry.

I turned off the lights
Walked into the night
And left you to sleep
On your rumpled sheets

TIME FLOATED

The patterns
Resemble art's

There is no logic here
At least none which
Philosophers would recognize:

We dreamt ourselves
To a different place,

Time floated on
Our feelings;

We saw the invisible
And the light, cast
No shadows, even
As it guided.

It is thus, that
God moves in mysterious ways,
His wonders to perform,

SCUTTLED LOVE

You'd wrung your heart dry
And hung your lies on the line

        for all to see

It wasn't true what I had heard
It wasn't true what I had thought
               and

I hadn't seen everything

Your heart you said wasn't there
You couldn't feel it
      So you scuttled love from within

Yesterday

I saw you standing on the corner
Your heart a begging bowl
You had given all you had
And had been left with a deadened soul

THE KINGDOM OF THE HEART

You caught a glimpse
        of the girlser
                in me

and wondered what
        it meant.

You admired
        my beautiful
                body,

as you took
    an oath of
            loyalty,

to the
    Kingdom of the Heart.

Years of self denial
and toil

had left you
    dried and parched,

but now your tears
        water the soil,

in the
        Kingdom of the Heart.

I held your lovely
                body,

its silk smooth
    skin affection starved,

then we sailed the sea of
        ecstasy,

to the
  Kingdom of the Heart.

We made love until
    dawn,

we loved that journey
    from the start,

our plans included
    our spawn;

(loyal subjects all)

in the
  Kingdom of the Heart.

I called your name
    and there was silence,

I wondered what had
    become of your heart.

I swore then; for you,
    I'd go the distance,

in the
  Kingdom of the Heart.

There was a tree,
      bough laden,

its fruits pretty and tart,

it grew in
    despair's garden,

in the
  Kingdom of the Heart.

I met a lonely traveler,

he proffered pearls
of wisdom
from the start,

but could offer me
no water

(to quench my thirst)

in the
Kingdom of the Heart.

'am thirsty! I called;

he had only food for
thought,

his words to me were like
gall,

in the
Kingdom of the heart.

My soul longed to
quench its thirst,

I found in the effort more art
than craft

and had I faltered,
would not my heart have burst,

in the
Kingdom of the Heart.

The sunlight bathed my
hopes,

your light flickered like
a distant star,

and I marveled at love's
                    scope,
in the
    Kingdom of the Heart.

NAKED IN THE DARK

You ran naked in the
          dark to the
                    light.

You had seen enough

and had tasted
          bitter fright.

Now it came to you.

It was true:
he was as
rough as had
been said and
without a clue.

Your heart had known
that despite its warming
you would not love him.
Your marriage vows were
turned in time to a worm.

II
The water showered
          on you,

your body relaxed
          and refreshed
          by its flow,

then you heard
          the door
ease off its hinges.

Now you know.

It begins.

It was not for
        loves' sake
or anything you had
            done.

It would all fall
    on your head
and if he could,
    strike you dumb.

You knew better and
held a secret he
    could not know:

though your skin
        could be broken
your heart was
beyond reach
and could not be taken.

III

Up ahead in the darkened
            room
they huddled, cowed by his
        will
and years later
    the stain he left
would linger,
    to mark his errant skill.

I had seen it flash
    in your eyes:

a sense of impending doom;

I reached for your heart
and found it weighted,
    heavy with gloom.

IV

He had tried his best
          with you

but could not fight his
          envy,

it gnawed his heart
          to know
that his would always be
          empty.

He marveled at your
          talent,

your gifts dazzled
          him,

but he lacked your
generosity of spirit

so could not puzzle,
          anger's whim.

A SONG OF MYSTERY

They sing a song of
          mystery
though only to
          those who
          cannot hear,
their language is bound
          in ecstasy
as they fly or
          land near.

Heaven's friends or
          unknown minions
we watch unknowing,
          their myriad missions.
Who can tell at
          journey's end
whither they fly as
          foe or friend.

"A little birdie told me"
piqued my curiosity;
I wondered then: what
          mission
seeks me each day
          before my ablutions.

I laid upon my bed,
each feathered whirl
a flutter of interest just
          ahead;
I knew then, another
          mystery of the world.

A flock of seven egrets
          flew formation;
feathered clouds across a blue
          sky,

two bumped, shrugged then
                    sung:
like you my friend,
            we only try.

They'll fly forever to
    land on Heaven's bough
and will walk on
                water;
carry aloft our heart's desires,
                    though,
we wouldn't think so.

Life is filled with
                mystery,
it surrounds us where'er
                    we may go,
all of life sings of ecstasy,
the inner voice tells no lies.

WE SIT TOGETHER

Is it real enough
        for you.

A military bearing
      hides an empty
         heart.
The mind,
      with not much more,
grapples with
        the vacuum of its
          knowing.

"I'd bend, if I could,
all of life to my will."

It's a fools' errand
but comforting
      nonetheless.

We sit and contemplate
        the setting sun,
it moves about its life
with a majestic indifference.

We fall prone to our feelings
and
    watch in consternation
        her fire-play.

We sit together
    to find comfort
        in our
little exercises: far from
    our pasts and
    alone together.

The Caricom whores
while away the time
listening to ennui's whispers.

On the beach, we congregate
to pay homage to ourselves
        and keep boredom at bay.
Her eyes shone brilliant
                and sad,
loneliness fingered her locks
    and guided her hand
            to her heart:
It's cold, she said
        and cowled it in black

Her eyes shone a pale blue
                solitude.

I know you, she said
        can you know me…

Is it real enough for you?
I'll be your minion
            if you can
        find my heart.

STRUGGLED TO KEEP FROM LEAPING

I looked into the abyss
and saw
my heart.

My mind struggled
to keep
from leaping.

Would I fly
if I tried.

I felt the burden
of the world
ease itself comfortable
in a corner
of my mind.

It sighed itself shut
and
floated away,
me in tow.

I drifted atop my
long lost dreams
and saw then
what I had not known:

nothing is ever lost
to the imagination!

I keened in despair
and heard my echo
startling my long dead dreams
to life.

Come and join us they laughed:

you slept for an eternity
while we were dreaming new worlds
into being.

ADIEU

You're no saint
      though you try.
You think it normal:
Though your heart is as
     wide as the sky;
Your shyness says
  it's all cordial.

I watched you walk away
      upon the water,
sailing to a not too
     distant shore.
I held our love high
     above my shoulder
and wondered why
  my heart felt sore.

You had spat at
      my feet
a fettered barb
which stung; even
     as I called you sweet-
heart. I took our love
     and daubed

my wound, as
  I turned
away from your
     mordant thrust.
You said I was petty,
     and burnt
me, as I watched your
     back, crust-

ed with my glare, drift away.
Now, I stand on the shore,
waiting for you to sway
me, as we settle this score.

You said you were
            sorry
but you had to go.
I said I would wait
            for ecstasy,
even if it couldn't be so.

We laugh, we cry
the pain always hurts
            just so;
then for loves sake
            must we try
and salve our wounds adieu.

HE LISTENS

He listens attentively
To his future plans
Being told to him.

""I'm beginning from scratch."

He had put all his heart
Into one basket, and lived
To see it; balanced on a
Kerchiefed head, being
Taken to market.

Heart's for sale;
The despair's deep
If you can bear it.
Broken or mended,
It's still a heart.

He had thought that:
Love is all you'd need;
But women didn't find
His kind of love – soft
And gentle – commanding
Enough, to melt their hearts.

His ideals, forged in
Christian piety had
Appeared merely
Decorous to the refined,
Foolish to the blind.

Yet he kept on at it:
Loving against all odds;
Not knowing that love,
Foolish love, can get
You your heart sold
At market from a worn basket.

His mettle had been burnished
By a too taut teaching which
Left no hunger for curiosity's sake;
His ideals stood him in good stead,
But only in his own mind; where
They mattered to no one else.

He needed guidance of the sort
That comes only too late – when nothing
Matters.

I told him of the hope
To be found in a distant land
And ever hopeful; but without
Curiosity, he accepted the offer
Of hope as assurance that his
Heart, though sold, could not be broken.

WHERE PLEASURE AND PAIN MEETS

You said the gesture
            was telling.

I had placed both hands
            on your back
and as I had been taught;
aimed for a relaxed passage.

It felt like me, painting,
            you said.

You held me tight. Here,
you said, is where
the pleasure and pain meet.

You paint my body
            and I shall
                  ask the questions.

The pressure releases,
but pleasure needs pain,
            so try again.

Tell me: how does
hurting precedes
            the pleasure.

I bent in ardent supplication
at your lovely body.

I kneaded the flesh I
felt and heard a grown
swivel from your lips.

You sighed and asked
the question I had heard
a thousand times:

How does love dance
in the palm of the hand.

I held your precious body.
You said
    you wanted it much deeper:
so deep that it would
take you beyond the
pain to that place
    called ecstasy,
where you longed to be.

You had not been
there before so could
not tell when the pain should
have ended and
pleasure's song begin.

You had grown accustomed
to the comforts of mortification.
You wanted the pain, to make you feel.

You could no longer tell
if it were pain or pleasure
or the pleasure of pain
        you wanted.
You wanted to feel,
    to know
that something – anything – mattered
        to you.

Pain was nearest at hand
and could be relied upon
to comfort you to the core;
so you begged for more
of what you knew
and had grown accustomed to.

AMONGST THE LILIES

You stood amongst the lilies,
your back straight, your gaze direct.
Your bed had not then been
abandoned by ardour's crèche.

You held within your palm
the promise of love.
It was a picture of happiness;
that was then, this is now.

You laid upon your bed,
your eyes silted for regretting.
You held my hand in yours,
it was firm and full of longing.

You said you would be gone for three weeks;
but it was time slipping away from your grasp.
I had loved you once but had come to regard
you with indifference. It's progress

of a sort I suppose: between love and indifference
slips a world of experience.

MOTHER SEA

The Sea. Mother of
           us all
wash me, bless my
              wishes.

"I am enjoying this"

You had sat, looking
           out at the waves;
feeling the wind
           run by you.

You had not known
           that this
         day, would be
   like this,
      just like this:

with your own flesh
        and blood

holding you taut
        against the
      pounding waves.

Just then you screamed;
it had been told to you
that this day would come,
when the sea would roll away
and you would stand alone.

You stood and recounted
        the sad tale:

You had loved
       and was
prepared to see it
           pass;

but waited patiently
for your time,
when your pen
would turn
cutlass.

We knew the story
well enough:
She had gone to live
with you
but love was still
born.

Your children, not
knowing why,
kept in touch. There
was caring, but love
was all but gone.

"This is my time"

They wanted to hear
your story, it was
new to them, but we
who had heard it,
wondered why it
needed to be told.

You felt the tug
that would
pull you down!

But, you stood firm,
your ground solid
with memories
as you confessed
to us all how love
had left you empty.

You looked young for
your age,

your eyes forlorn and lifeless,

you were sustained by
        embers of rage

as you waited the end
            under duress.

Free me, Jesus, you cried:
your eyes turned heavenward,

but we who knew you, tried
to tell: it would be hell for your words.

We follow along in your wake
oblivious to all but your cruel whim.

We had cried but our tears could not slake
or sooth our welt creased skin.

It was always for love
you said: I hurt out
of the kindness of my heart.

We stood our ground in hope
that it was more than despair.

I BENT MY KNEES IN SUPPLICATION

I bent my knees
      in supplication
and called upon
        the deep,
I wanted to find
      that place
where life is as still
        as the sleep

of the dead.

You, who sing
      in the dark!

I have none of the answers,
        you said.
You pulled the strings
      that would
    burst my heart;

but I know more
      of it than you.

You hid yourself
within the shadows
of your heart.
It folded upon itself
a thousand times and
left you hidden in the dark.

From the throne of darkness
you preached forth. A whisper
here and there always did the trick.

I drifted away from your
shivering touch
as we approached your Styx.

You tried to walk upon the water
but it could not stand you ashen sole.

She rolled away from your touch
and closed her eyes to your soul.

You thought that you were that powerful
that water, even water, would stand for you.

You had not learned in all your years
that only love, can make you light.

There were two of us from yesterday,
now only one of us is here to stay;

where you shall retire, would
you see yourself reflected in the sky?

The hope is always forlorn
when we hesitate at loves door.

Come, look into my heart, it's
as wide as the sky and full of hope

ONCE WHEN WE WERE YOUNG

(FOR GWENETH HANLEY 1946 – 2006)

Once, when we were young,
the future seemed limitless
            in her promise:

we'd sail through life,
confident that
        even in the
                roughest seas,
we'd come through unbowed.

Youth held our skin taut,
our eyes saw all and more,
we sang for joy and our
tears dried, before they'd fall.

We were happy.

Then life would intervene,
to remind us that
each one of us has
an appointment to keep.

We see it every day:
Someone leaves;
and in leave—taking
reminds us that
one day our time
too shall come.

Graying hair, a paunch
            too far,
nephews and nieces
who remind us we
can never be alone,
come between us
and our appointment.
They keep us engaged
in the show
until its time to go.

We make a ritual
of our leave—taking:
we remember, only the
good deeds: what
of our lives touched
and sustained others.

We flatter ourselves
that time shall have been
kind to us.

But, the consistent
heartbeat in all of our
                lives is:

The circle completed.

We see it a thousand times
and it's the same everyday
                and everywhere:

Over there, we shall
meet again; it seems
too much of a shock
to let go and to do
so without hope.

So, we sing of meeting
on the beautiful shore,

we pray that our souls
would rest in eternal peace,

or at least, find rest
from earthly chore.

We live in hope that
there is something
more to life than the
finality of death

and so, we create a
Saviour who rose on
the third day and assures
us too, that, if He, the
'Son of Man' can live
again, then so can we!

We live and in living
rejoice, for we believe
(we cannot know)
that here, when we
depart, our barque shall
alight on some golden shore.

But are we sure: there is
no certainty in what happens
after death; but we hope; as
when we were young, for the best.

Our hope sustains us.

HOLD SWAY

It was unexpected
and took you by
        surprise.

You swayed under
       its burden

and thought your shock
        would suffice.

It kept you up wondering
where you had gone wrong.
There was no telling
where such rage had grown strong

II

I am lonely and
with no one
to take me
      seriously,

so I wander my
    path alone.

I have discovered
that the absence of
caring leads me to
slip away from home.

III

You thought your
    mind made up:
he was the one whom
      I tried
to show the way, but
sometimes the seed
falls and takes root
in barren soil.

I wondered myself at
the outburst; a cry
for help is always
an easy fix.

Forgiveness, you said,
            is important,
yet he held his pain
    close to his heart.

IV
Your heart bleeds
at its betrayal.
It cries when left alone.

V
My mind turned away
from what I thought
was mine and
looked to a
            distant shore.

You're strong and
will survive the passage.
It's only life
if you see it that way.

So, let it be
            and
                hold sway.

PICTURE PERFECT

The photos were
   compelling,

we stood alone
   together:

me, happy and smiling;

you, shy within
  your shell.

We were well posed.

I engaged the lens
and smiled as to
  a friend
and
 slipped open a
window to my soul.

It stopped me in my tracks,
spellbound by what I saw.

I had not known until
then how happy I could be.

He looks as young as
your son and saved

by grace, or so they said.
I knew it was being with you
which renewed my lease:

now I know;
now I can sing;
now I feel.

Life can never sting
those who truly love.

The eyes reveal so much,

I'm taken aback. I search
in them for a clue and fall

headlong into swimming
for my life.

It makes me happy to know
that with you by my side,

I see ahead in the distance
the hint of things to come;

they reach us with that look
that says: happiness can be yours.

WHAT SHALL IT BE

I laid upon my bed
        lost in thought,
The ceiling shimmered
        under my gaze
as I saw before me the
the shape of things to come.

I had wondered at your
            surmise,
which in time seemed
so cleverly crafted:
the door had been opened
to the possibility of an ending
no one wanted.

You needed to protect your heart
in case your body could not
bear the burden of our hopes,
it seemed reasonable enough.

But I wondered: why that path;
why not hope for the best?
Was it something deep within you?
Was it a doubt you could not shake?

It seemed less than wise
to want an ending,
even as you planned
for a bright future,

which would claim our hearts.
Let's just be friends
would be our love's epitaph,
'though our hearts were
capable of so much more.

You preferred to live with
the surety of regret
than the uncertainty of love.

It pays to know the score.
It pays to believe.
I kept my heart for myself,
braced against the faint hope

for that day, when I shall
hear you say: we're no more.
You would then make clear
all the claims you had only hinted at:

I was too perfect;
I like to have my own way;
this relationship is too draining;
it's taking all my energy.

I had heard between your lines
an unacknowledged doubt.
I pressed my heart into service
knowing that it may not last.

I began to look to a distant shore
to be safe on solid ground, for that day
when, I shall hear you say:
Lets just be friends.

FOR THE MOMENT

Dappled sunlight
   on brown skin.
The leaves played
   in the wind.
They sketched fleeting shadows
on the dirty window pane.
I followed the arc of her flow
until it came to rest,
gently, in my mind.

I floated, feeling in my heart
every flutter of shadowed leaves
and came to beach
on the shore of my feelings.
I had waited an eternity
to arrive on this scene.

The wind stops and sighs
herself shut.
The leaves wait for her
to puff her next gust;
wondering, where the play shall end.

In the sky, I glimpse
a thousand shapes
of things to come
through the gently
swaying leaves.

A dance now. Branches
keep their distance as they
loll to the call of the flowing wind:
A stately chaconne or a rollback
to a big drum.
A bird breaks in on the
scene but is indifferent
to the music.
It has errands to fly.

The dance shall continue
for an eternity
or for as long as we can stay
to see the light.

The line on the pane
slowly descends;
shadows following
the sun for respite.

They are patient
for they know: only
for so long can she
toy with us like this
before she must sink
below the waves,
to slake her thirst;
we shall pine for her,
but only for a night,
before she calls us
again to come parse her light.

THE BREADTH OF YOUR HIPS

One could see
in the shape of the lips,
a memory from so long ago
which time had let slip.

The voice had changed
too. You had cried too often
in pain and not enough for joy.
Your eyes had been made soft

by the scattered light of experience.
You remembered me! You sauntered
forth; teasing out of me a generation's
worth of memories. You'd haunted

me a lifetime and now, I felt
the warmth I had longed for
so many years ago, singe the
door to my past shut. For-

getting wouldn't be that easy.
We spoke and rolled over thirty
years of remembering and letting go.
Seeing you now made me thirsty

for that night, so long ago, when
you had promised to take me
through the gate. Only later would I
come to know that ecstasy

which laid beyond the gate.
But, as often as
I had entered, I would
remember you. It was

your voice; the way it
glided me to a stop
within myself. I could, or
so it seemed, crop

nothing of my feelings
once you spoke. I had,
for all of these years,
remembered the hard

curl of your lips; the look
in your eyes and the shape
of your hips in your fourth
form uniform. Had I erased,

or tried to, the memory
of the night we sat outside
the Methodist Church and
made promises we'd slide

pass; I couldn't have lived.
I'd kept deep within
my heart the plan: it sustained
me; even against time's withering

hand. We'd meet later that
night, but, when I had returned,
you were gone. I held the
possibilities in my, no, burnt
them into my heart and they
would have stayed there
forever, had you not held me
yesterday. I surrendered care

to your touch and, you could
not have known how, after all these
many years, I noticed the breadth
of your hips and wondered.

THERE IS NO PROOF.

There is no proof, there is no evidence;
There is no faith, no things unseen to come:
Only me and you, bound in deference;
Doing all that it takes, what needs to be done.

We go to church to pray and learn new lies:
We tell new lies to avoid drab, cold truths.
The dulled pain is real, the suffering gibes.
Your voice, tears the bark off, down to its roots.

You sing of a lover who's far away.
Your every word a fear, a hope forlorn
Your plans – the melody cries – will hold sway.
Every verse, a hope against the stillborn.

Oh love, unchanging love, why do we sing?
To staunch the heart and stay truth's searing sting.

THE FLESH WAS WEAK
FOR DONALD FLEMMING

I did bad things,
Caused pain, gave hurt,
Sinned my soul and caused tears to flow.
I knew all the lies,
Told them well,
Vied against the current
Drank from many wells.

I knew I was wrong,
But told myself:
It's all for love!

But I lied
And knew the truth, even as I knelt.

There were flowered kisses
    And candled nights.
Sweet-hued words, served to thrill
            Green appetites.

It was all a dream
Or so I pretended.

The lies grew longer
More empty,
As I grew older.

Between your thighs
I had begun the journey,
The search
For meaning.

(Or at least, that's what I told myself)

But, I knew all along, all along, it was
Me and you and the truth:

The flesh was weak.
But oh, so sweet.

NOW THAT I KNOW

Let me twist in the wind, fall to my knees
I knew the reasons why, but oh! The lies
Were sweet and I yielded, knowing the truth
But preferring the lie I lived, holding
Fast, running fast against my past, hoping
Somehow that it would all end well for me.

The things I did, the acts, had their moment;
Fleeting, sensuous, rewarding , but oh
They added up; one by one: weighed me down
One by one to burden each step I took

If only I had known…what I do now
What difference would it have made I ask.
I ask, I ask, I ask, I ask. Now that I know…

LAY OF THE LAND

FOR AL MALONGA

I think I'm beginning to understand
The lay of the land: how clouds shade trees
How the earth rolls away from a dank sky
And the heart slips away from those who tease.

I had thought the answers were close at hand
That we could do it all in jeans and tees
But you on your back, wrapped to match the sky
Whispered: with love, the journey never ends.

CPSIA information can be obtained
at www.ICGtesting.com
Printed in the USA
LVOW03s2237060717
540518LV00001B/2/P